CONTEMPORARY MUSICIANS
AND THEIR MUSIC™

Dixie Chicks

Brett Mitchells

ROSEN
PUBLISHING®
New York

For Doris

Published in 2009 by The Rosen Publishing Group, Inc.
29 East 21st Street, New York, NY 10010

Library of Congress Cataloging-in-Publication Data

Mitchells, Brett.
Dixie Chicks / Brett Mitchells.—1st ed.
    p. cm.—(Contemporary musicians and their music)
Includes bibliographical references (p. 46) and index.
ISBN-13: 978-1-4042-1817-8 (library binding)
ISBN-13: 978-1-4358-5125-2 (pbk)
ISBN-13: 978-1-4042-7870-7 (6 pack)
1. Dixie Chicks (Musical group)—Juvenile literature. 2. Country musicians—United States—Biography—Juvenile literature. I. Title.
ML3930.D58M53 2008
781.642092'2—dc22
[B]
                                                                    2008005602

Manufactured in Malaysia

On the cover: A photograph of the Dixie Chicks.

Contents

Introduction

There would be years of struggle. There would be controversy. But through many hardships, the Dixie Chicks would stick to their guns and win the heart of America.

The Dixie Chicks have sold more records than any female group in any musical genre. Their music has sold 30.5 million CDs, cassettes, and records. That's more albums than either 'N Sync or Nirvana!

But success didn't come easy. While you may know the Chicks as a sassy country trio consisting of Natalie Maines, Martie Maguire, and Emily

Before they became a great success, the Dixie Chicks entertained crowds on Dallas street corners.

Robison, the group didn't start out that way. Before Maines was a member of the Dixie Chicks, there was another singer who worked with Maguire and Robison. There was even a fourth member. Years before the Chicks entertained crowds at the Super Bowl, there was a time in their lives when they performed on street corners wearing cowgirl costumes. During these lean years, they took almost any gig just to get by. And before they were interviewed by the likes of Diane Sawyer, for example, the Chicks were strictly local talents—the darlings of Dallas.

The Dixie Chicks' story involves hard beginnings and unexpected setbacks. They were talented musicians determined to succeed. They never gave up on their dream. They took chances. And they were also willing to make hard sacrifices to get national attention.

Chapter One

The Hatching of the Dixie Chicks

Martie Erwin was five years old when she began playing classical violin in Addison, Texas. Her sister Emily began playing violin when she was seven. But since Martie was so fine on the fiddle, Emily took to playing banjo because it seemed like a rebellious thing to do. After all, how many girls picked up a banjo?

Martie had an accomplished fiddle style by the time she was twelve years old. She would go on to win third place in the 1989 National Fiddle Championships. Emily was self-taught. She learned banjo by tracking the chord progressions in books.

The sisters were encouraged to take an interest in music by their parents. Their father, Paul Erwin, was a passionate country

Emily taught herself how to play the banjo by tracking chord progressions in books.

music fan and the headmaster of a private school. Their mother, Barbara Trask, was a classical violinist who taught at a private school. While the Erwin girls didn't grow up with a lot of money, their parents' jobs enabled them to get a private school education.

This schooling resulted in Martie and Emily meeting two other kids who would have a significant impact on their musical development. Their music teachers partnered the Erwin girls with Sharon and Troy Gilchrist. The sister and brother were already performing as a bluegrass duo, and the Erwins and the Gilchrists soon discovered their mutual love of bluegrass. (Once, they even sneaked away from school to attend the Walnut Valley Festival, a bluegrass festival in Kansas!)

Martie started playing the violin when she was five years old. She won third place in the 1989 National Fiddle Championships.

With Sharon Gilchrist on the mandolin and Troy Gilchrist learning how to flat-pick on a mammoth guitar bigger than his body, the young Erwin sisters finally had two devoted musicians to help them hone their talents. Sid Gilchrist, father to Sharon and Tony, didn't know if this budding quartet would succeed.

"I just drive the bus," he was fond of saying, according to the Dixie-Chicks.com Web site.

From 1982 to 1988, this energetic quartet of teenagers, who came to be known as the Blue Night Express, entertained audiences while they also developed their bluegrass skills. They played festivals. They jammed with the legendary fiddler Mark O'Connor. They learned how to write and perform music.

Taking It to the Streets

Eventually, the time came for the Gilchrists to go off to college. Martie and Emily decided to disband the Blue Night Express, leaving them somewhat uncertain about how to proceed in their musical careers. Martie was nineteen and Emily was sixteen, but the girls were determined not to spend their summers waiting tables.

So, in 1989, with the Blue Night Express dissolved, the Erwin sisters found two other musicians to perform with: Robin Macy (on guitar) and Laura Lynch (on bass). Macy was a sixth-grade math teacher who often played bluegrass for her students. When she wasn't playing her guitar in the classroom, she was playing at bluegrass festivals. Lynch had worked as stockbroker. After a baby and a divorce, she was looking for a new start. She began taking guitar lessons and attending bluegrass festivals, where she met Macy. Both Macy and Lynch were ten years older than the Erwin girls. This age difference would have a major impact on the Dixie Chicks' future.

The new quartet's first performance was on a West End street corner in Dallas. The four women were dressed in cowgirl outfits. When they emerged from Emily's Caprice Classic with an array of instruments, wild cowboy hats, and colorful skirts and blouses, their striking presence stopped traffic. It was entirely unexpected to see four women playing country music—a musical genre dominated by men. To their considerable surprise, the quartet made $375 in one hour.

The new band didn't yet have a name, but after hearing the Little Feat classic "Dixie Chicken" on the radio one day on the way to the street corner, they took the name Dixie Chicks. The name stuck.

The Chicks made their first club appearance at Poor David's Pub and began performing at other Dallas clubs, supermarket openings throughout Texas, and just about any venue that would have them. Dallas locals were delighted to hear the Chicks make a radio appearance on the NPR program *The Prairie Home Companion*.

But what nobody knew was that this was just the beginning of an ever-shifting career that would lead the young women into new musical directions, an unexpected change in lineup, and a controversy that would dramatically alter the public's perception of them.

Chapter Two

The Big Break

The Dixie Chicks wanted fame and they wanted it badly, but national attention continued to elude them. The group kept on playing all sorts of venues, including barbeques, state fairs, and corporate parties. A year after their fateful debut on a street corner, they sang a local jingle for a McDonald's sandwich. (Ironically, one member of the group was a vegetarian at the time.)

In 1990, the Chicks were named the Best Band at the Telluride Bluegrass Festival. Three years later, they were voted the Best Local Country Band by the *Dallas Morning News*. They continued to perform regularly at their favorite local haunts (Poor David's Pub and Uncle Calvin's Coffeehouse). Everywhere they played, the Chicks impressed audiences with their musicianship and complex harmonizing.

Early in their career, the Chicks wowed eager crowds at Poor David's Pub and Uncle Calvin's Coffeehouse.

"Some man introduced us on stage one time," recalled Robin Macy in the *Dallas Morning News*, "and he said, 'You are not going to believe these women. They are so pretty, and they play like men.'"

Ups and Downs

If there was an area where the Dixie Chicks perhaps needed some improvement, it was in their stage show. "The Dixie Chicks from Dallas were musically flawless," noted a critic for the *Austin*

American-Statesman, "but [they] need more stage presence and focus to their performance." They were declared "run-of-the-mill" by another *Austin American-Statesman* music critic, and a *Washington Post* reporter wrote that the Chicks' "lyrics and harmonies were almost uniformly lost in the tubby sound mix."

Despite these less-than-flattering reviews, the Warner Brothers record label responded positively to the Dixie Chicks after a performance of theirs in Nashville, Tennessee. However, Warner Brothers wanted the Chicks to add a drummer to their lineup, and drums were not normally included in the traditional bluegrass that the band was interested in playing. Therefore, the Warner Brothers deal fell through, and in 1990, the Chicks decided to put out an album on their own independent label, Little Red Hen. The album, titled *Thank Heaven for Dale Evans*, was composed of both original songs and covers. The Chicks sold the album out of their van. (They also sold T-shirts that read, "The rooster crows, but the hen delivers.") Eventually, the band managed to sell thirteen thousand copies. "We've gone aluminum!" cried Macy, as quoted in the *Austin American-Statesman*.

Around this time the Dixie Chicks had high-profile perform-ances at the Kennedy Center and at the first official reception for the mayor of Dallas. The Chicks also began to shift away from bluegrass by adding a drummer, a University of North Texas graduate named Tom Van Schiuk. They also signed up with a Nashville booking agency, Buddy Lee Attractions, becoming the first band to sign to the agency without a manager or a recording contract. And they were making money! "Very few acts can go in a few years from working for the cover charge to $2,500 plus per show," said David Card, the owner of Poor David's Pub, in the *Dallas Morning News*. Emily bought a mini-trampoline so that the Chicks could get their blood circulating before performing a show. When they weren't performing, they sewed more beads and sequins onto their cowgirl outfits and made business calls.

In 1992, the Dixie Chicks set out on the Fish & Chicks Tour with the band Trout Fishing in America. More than a few commentators continued to express surprise that the Chicks hadn't been snatched up by a major record label. "Any fool can see that these four women (augmented by drummer Tom Vanischuik [sic]) have got it, that indescribable wow that separates the chosen few from the pretenders," wrote a reporter for the *Dallas Morning News*. "Although saddled with the worst band name since the Doobie Brothers, the Dixie Chicks impart the sort of musical gifts that turn audience members into armchair record execs. They seem like a can't-miss project."

Evolution of the Band

In 1992, the Dixie Chicks used different instrumentation for their second album, *Little Ol' Cowgirl*. They hired Larry Seyer, a producer from Austin, Texas, who had worked with Ray Benson and Asleep at the Wheel. Seyer produced the Chicks' album with a more polished western swing sound. *Little Ol' Cowgirl* made its debut at a party that benefited Foster Child Advocate Services at Dick's Last Resort. The Chicks continued to sell their albums out of a little Samsonite suitcase.

After the release of *Little Ol' Cowgirl*, and having made significant changes to their sound, the Dixie Chicks began playing more gigs across the United States. But all was not well with the group. Macy was not happy with their new musical direction. Unlike the other three band members, she had not wanted to go mainstream country. She decided to leave the group to go back to teaching. To inform the public of her decision, she handwrote four hundred notices and sent them to fans and the press.

"Success means becoming a mainstream country act, and the three of them are pretty excited about pursuing a commercial country career," said Macy in the *Austin American-Statesman*. "But I've always been a singer/songwriter-type, and I love Celtic music and bluegrass and lots of stuff. Where they were going didn't suit my philosophical bent, so I decided to let them pursue it."

With three Chicks left, the band continued to promote itself, getting its single "I've Got a Heart That Can" into airplay

RHINESTONES AND FRINGE

The Dixie Chicks' eccentric cowgirl costumes were a source of minor controversy for them. Some thought the costumes relegated the Chicks to a novelty act. Others thought the costumes were fun and gave the band an instantly recognizable look. Either way, the Chicks kept the costumes for several years and spent long hours working on them.

They scoured through many shops to find fringed chaps, vintage western shirts, and, of course, cowboy boots. Any flea market that came through town was a source for apparel. They employed a designer, Laurie Rudd, to alter thrift-shop clothing, but they also weren't above modifying cowgirl wear themselves. "We customize old western shirts with beading," Martie Maguire told Kendall Morgan of the *Dallas Morning News*. "If they're really in bad shape, we cut the sleeves off or put a pin over a big stain. We'll dye things that aren't the right color. We'll make it work because it might be a while until you find another find."

on a few Dallas/Fort Worth radio stations. All of their hard work paid off. In 1993, the Chicks secured a gig to play at President Bill Clinton's inaugural ball, and they headed off to California for even more touring. "Hard to believe this is the group that played a hair salon opening three years ago for $75. Their rate now: $5,000," observed *Dallas Morning News* columnist Helen Bryant.

In addition to political functions, the Chicks also began playing more high-profile venues. They opened for the Richardson Symphony Orchestra on June 12, 1993. That same month, they spent one weekend opening for Tammy Wynette in Branson, Missouri. Their costumes became so rhinestone-heavy that they began to set off metal detectors in airports. Even their backstage treatment began to improve. "We got the best meal we've eaten since we left Dallas," gushed Laura Lynch to a reporter for the *Boston Herald* when the Chicks hit a hot club in Boston. "There were fresh flowers in our dressing room, and no chicken wire around the stage. We don't get treated any better than this!"

Branching Out

In 1993, the Dixie Chicks released their third album, *Shouldn'ta Told You That*. While they had been enjoying a larger degree of success, they had not been able to achieve the sort of full-blown, nationwide radio play that they desired. Therefore, their third album saw them returning to their country roots while likewise offering a few carrots to tempt the great horse of radio. "We've written several songs just for the radio," Lynch told a *Dallas Morning News* reporter about the album. The Erwin sisters also joked with the reporter that they were spending so much time working on the album in the studio that they had to bring food and pillows along.

The Dixie Chicks started touring other countries. The group played two sold-out concerts in Zurich, Switzerland. They collaborated with the Fort Worth Dallas Ballet, an idea that came from the artistic director of the dance troupe. "He said he thought this might increase exposure to different audiences for both groups," they told the *Dallas Morning News*. The original idea for this one-off partnership was for the Chicks to pen original tunes, but there wasn't enough time. So, their preexisting songs became the basis for a new ballet called *All the Right Women*. Margaret Putnam, of the *Dallas Morning News*, described the Chicks starting off the set with a mad medley of tunes. From there, seven cowboys sauntered out, "hooking thumbs in belt and taking all the usual cowboy postures."

Third party candidate Ross Perot was among many of the political heavyweights that the Chicks entertained.

The Dixie Chicks also played some major concerts for Texas politicians, including one with Ross Perot. Years before future band member Natalie Maines would say harsh words about President George W. Bush, the Chicks played "a very sophisticated hillbilly party" that was attended by George and Laura Bush. In a description bearing the echo of later events, the Dixie Chicks proved to be the band "most perplexing to the dancing Republicans," according to Helen Bryant of the *Dallas Morning News*.

Around this time, trouble came for the Dixie Chicks when a U-Haul truck containing $22,000 worth of their sound equipment was stolen. To make matters worse, the equipment was not insured. "It's pretty devastating for us," Lynch told Bryant. "We're going to have to rent everything now, whenever we play."

The Chicks called sound dealers and warned them not to buy the stolen goods.

There remained some prospects for the Chicks signing on with a major record label, but nobody was biting in the hard and choppy waters of the music business. The group continued to get gigs, even if it meant literally slipping through the cracks. At one show at a boot store, Lynch fell through the stage. "Everybody kept playing, and I was just a singing head sticking out," she told the *Knoxville News-Sentinel*. "I'm glad nobody had a video camera."

Meanwhile, Martie got married, taking the last name Seidel. She became the first of the Chicks to walk down the aisle while in the band. (She was divorced a few years later but was married again, taking the name Maguire.) Marriage, however, did not put a halt to their diligence. "She's going on her honeymoon, then she's coming back to work," Lynch told Alan Peppard of the *Dallas Morning News*.

The Changing Face of the Dixie Chicks

Then came a startling development, one that would finally give the Chicks the success that they had spent four hard and ambitious years working for. But it would not be without human cost. Laura

Lynch, who had helped to secure the Chicks' performance at the Clinton inaugural gala, was asked to leave by Emily and Martie. Lynch, at thirty-seven years old, was "too old" to be a Dixie Chick. Emily was twenty-three. Martie was twenty-five. It was the dark side of show business. They needed someone younger. "It can't really be characterized as a resignation," said Lynch in the *Dallas Morning News*. "There are three Dixie Chicks, and I'm only one." At the time, Lynch said that she understood the reasons. But she would cry over this for the next six months.

Six months after Lynch's dismissal, the Chicks would have a record deal with a new singer. They would begin their stratospheric climb into the big time, with Lynch's and Macy's early contributions unmentioned in later interviews. Lynch would later leave the music business for good. Even though she missed out on the Dixie Chicks' great financial success, Lynch did find unexpected riches elsewhere. She later married a man named Mac Tull, who had the remarkable fortune to win $26.87 million in the Texas Lottery.

The Dixie Chicks' new singer was Natalie Maines, the daughter of noted steel-guitar legend Lloyd Maines, who had played on two of the Chicks' independent albums. The Chicks had frequently gone to dinner at the Maines house, and Natalie Maines had

Upon Laura Lynch's exit, the talented and tough-talking Natalie Maines made her entrance. She helped to catapult the Chicks to success.

become friends with Emily and Martie. Maines's family had a tradition of harmonizing together on Christmas Eve. And she often pretended to be the cartoon character Betty Boop, sitting on her granddad's lap and singing "Santa Baby."

Upon graduating from high school, Natalie Maines had won a vocal scholarship to the Berklee School of Music, in Boston, Massachusetts. Her audition tape had, in fact, included a song written by Robison and Maguire called "You Were Mine," even though she was more interested in singing jazz. Maines's stay at the Berklee School of Music lasted only one semester. Upon returning home to Texas, she studied commercial music at South Plains College before the two Chicks offered her the job as their new singer.

Maines would prove to be a fiery, controversial figure for the Chicks. The first thing she objected to was the cowgirl costumes. Right off the bat she told them, "I dig your music, but I'm not wearing stupid clothes," reported the *Boston Globe*. But Maines had good looks and the ability to yodel as well as sing. Maguire and Robison signed her on.

With the new lineup, not only did the Chicks finally have the big-label support that they had long craved, but they also began to draw larger crowds. The group sang "The Star-Spangled Banner" in three-part harmony in front of an audience of fifty thousand at a Texas Rangers game. An LED flag blew in the breeze. The fans let loose a stunning array of cheers. This was one of the first indicators of mass audience approval.

Hitting the Big Time

Recording began on the fourth Dixie Chicks album, *Wide Open Spaces*, in February 1997, with veteran Nashville producer Paul Worley coproducing. The Chicks' music began to emphasize a funky country sound that relied more on slide guitar, harmonizing, and dobro. "We want to be successful and get on the radio," said Maguire in *Tulsa World*. "You've got to play by the rules if you want to make it a career, and we're not so thick-headed that we

The Chicks traded in cowgirl costumes for slick platinum-blond locks.

can't take advice from the business side of things, you know. They want to make sure we're in it for the long haul, and right now, we're just groovin' on it."

A critic for the *Dallas Morning News* described the *Wide Open Spaces* song "You Were Mine" as "ultra-commercial, a smooth, seamless love song not unlike hits by Reba McIntire." The sound wasn't the only thing that had changed. The eccentric cowgirl costumes were traded in for a sleek new image involving platinum-blond tresses. Many people suggested that the revamped Chicks were country's answer to the Spice Girls. "People draw comparisons from what they know, and there haven't been too many trios like us," said Maguire in the *Sarasota Herald-Tribune*. "Wilson-Phillips we wouldn't have minded so much, but the Spice Girls?"

Whatever their mainstream faults, audiences loved the new Dixie Chicks. This fact helped the Chicks eventually sign a six-album recording contract with Sony Nashville, beginning with *Wide Open Spaces*. Sony had such faith in the Chicks that it revived the old Monument label, which had been the home for legendary singers Dolly Parton and Roy Orbison.

Not long after all this, in May 1997, Natalie Maines became the second Chick to get married, marrying bass player Michael Tarabay. Meanwhile, their audiences continued to mushroom. "The shows are a lot bigger," said Emily. "Our crowds have quadrupled. And a lot of it is fans our age that we feel like we want to relate to and can relate to." At the 1998 New Faces Show, the Chicks scored the highest out of all the bands. People were finally recognizing their distinct sound of dobro, fiddle, and harmonies. The Dixie Chicks were climbing their way up the vine leading to fame and fortune.

Chapter Three

Success and Controversy

For their fourth album, *Wide Open Spaces*, the Dixie Chicks had tested the songs on their growing concert audiences and used their reaction to decide which ones to include. Upon its release, the album sold 72,000 copies, according to SoundScan, and 380,000 copies were shipped to stores. It debuted on the Billboard charts at No. 17, the highest Billboard ranking for a country group since 1991. The Chicks were the only band in 1998 to have two singles enter the Top 15 on the country charts, and they were the only band to see their album sales increase eight weeks in a row. *Wide Open Spaces* had exceeded Sony's expectations.

This success led to games. For every number-one single or album, the Dixie Chicks promised to tattoo a tiny little chicken foot atop their toes. The first single, "I Can Love You Better," hit number seven on the Hot Country Singles & Tracks charts. But the second single, "There's Your Trouble," hit number one. Two additional singles also reached the number-one spot. It wouldn't be too long before the women would run out of toes!

The Chicks were nominated for two Country Music Association Awards: Best Vocal Group and the Horizon Award, a special prize reserved for newcomers. They won both awards. They won the Best New Country Artist category at the 26th annual American Music Awards. *Wide Open Spaces* also earned two Grammies: one for Best Country Performance by a Duo or Group with Vocal, and one for Best Country Album. (To everybody's surprise, the

GOOD-BYE TO THE OLD RV

As the Dixie Chicks hit the big time, some of the staples of their old lives necessarily fell by the wayside. One of these was the old RV that they had toured in and sold all their CDs from. It was traded in for a new bus with a bright Pepto Bismol–pink interior. The old vehicle was given away at the Fun Fair in Nashville, Tennessee. There would be no more broken TV. No more touring in an RV without a bathroom. No more selling self-released CDs from a Samsonite suitcase.

Wide Open Spaces earned the Chicks two Grammies, beating out big-time country artists Garth Brooks and Shania Twain.

Chicks had beaten out Garth Brooks and Shania Twain for the latter honor.) As the group added more shiny trophies to their mantles, Dallas locals were amused. They had watched the Chicks for years and now they were regarded as "new" by this national audience. "[T]he group is definitely old hat to the folks around town who bought the three albums before *Wide Open Spaces* hit the big time," wrote one *Dallas Morning News* reporter.

The Chicks were booked to sing "Stand by Your Man" in an Academy of Country Music tribute to Tammy Wynette. They were no longer an opening act for this country icon but a band blooming into legendary status in its own right.

Wide Open Spaces went platinum. Then it went double platinum. Then it sold three million copies! One year after its release, this "debut" Dixie Chicks album was quadruple platinum. And it would go on to sell even more. "This first one has been such a success," Maines told the *Dallas Morning News*, "and we really don't know what it is that we did. We just know that we picked songs we liked and made them our own. We know that we made the best album we could."

In April 1999, in the midst of all this success, Emily Erwin married Charlie Robison at the Cibolo Creek Ranch. It was a family-and-friends affair, and the Chicks played "Cowboy, Take Me Away" at the wedding.

The Price of Success

With the Dixie Chicks' greater success came the pressure to tone down their country sound in order to cross further into mainstream music. Television stations asked the Chicks to reshoot their videos without fiddles and steel guitars. They refused. During the summer of 1999, they became the first country act to join Lilith Fair, a concert celebrating women in music. "We're doing what we want to do, we're playing what we want to play, we're looking like we want to look, [and] we're saying what we want to say," said Maines in the *Buffalo News*.

Meanwhile, the Chicks continued recording songs for their new album. Their rendition of the Supremes song "You Can't

Hurry Love" appeared in the 1999 Julia Roberts film *Runaway Bride*. A music video followed; it depicted the Chicks floating in a punch bowl with oversized fruit. For the new album, they once again enlisted top tunesmiths from Nashville—including Buddy Miller and Patty Griffin—to write songs. "We all wrote about fifty songs," said Maguire on the BPI Entertainment News Wire, "and we picked only five of them for the album, so we're definitely very objective about it. I'm just glad everybody got something on there because it would be difficult if one had surfaced as a better writer than the others."

The working title of the new album was *Sin Wagon*, but it was changed to *Fly* and was released in October

In 1999, the Chicks were asked to tone down their country sound. They refused.

1999. *Wide Open Spaces* still continued to drift in and out of the Billboard Top 10 while *Fly* went on to sell some ten million units. *Fly* became that rare diamond album in the rough world of the music industry. The Chicks were now selling as well as the Backstreet Boys and 'N Sync. *Fly* debuted in the number-one spot on the Billboard 200 and spawned nine singles, including "Cowboy, Take Me Away" and "Without You." There was also the revenge song, "Goodbye Earl," about two high schoolers who plot to kill an abusive husband. The song's daring lyrics signaled a new attraction to controversy.

On August 29, 2001, the Dixie Chicks filed a lawsuit against Sony. They claimed that they had been defrauded of $4 million in profits. Meanwhile, they appeared before California legislators to discuss a statute that bound musicians to long-term contracts. "Yeah, we thought we were businesswomen at the time," said Maines in an NBC News interview, thinking of how the Chicks had thrown themselves into the mess. "And really the problem is not just with Sony. It's with the entire music industry. And new artists don't have an option but to sign the first contract that is put in their direction. And everyone around you will say, 'Oh, it's just standard, it's just normal.' And that's all true. And we just happened to get to a point where we had success and we had leverage, and we could stand up for ourselves and fight a battle that we felt very strongly in doing so." By the following summer, the lawsuit with Sony was resolved.

New Successes, New Sounds

After the September 11, 2001, terrorist attacks on the World Trade Center and the Pentagon, the Dixie Chicks were among the bands that took part in America: Tribute to Heroes. This was a concert that raised money for victims of the terrorist attacks. The Chicks contributed the well-received "I Believe in Love," which some saw as a significant change in their musical direction.

The song "I Believe in Love" was not their only change in musical direction. The Chicks next album, *Home*, most certainly was, even for a band with more departures than an airport terminal in the dead of winter. There were still the harmonies. Maguire still played the fiddle. Robison still played the banjo and dobro. But the electric guitars and drums had been toned down for a mainstream bluegrass future. At the same time, the Chicks relied on noncommercial songwriters for the first time, and this was the first CD since their early days that they had recorded in Texas. One of the new songs, "Long Time Gone," was a thinly veiled attack on the music industry.

Before raising a political ruckus, the Chicks found their way into American hearts at Super Bowl XXXVII.

But if the Chicks were showing signs of rebelling against the world of mainstream music, their record sales didn't reflect it. The album went on to sell six million copies. The Chicks followed up this success by playing Super Bowl XXXVII in 2003 and appearing that same year at the Grammy Awards.

The Insult Heard Around the World

On March 10, 2003, the Dixie Chicks encountered an entirely new level of fame, but for entirely unexpected reasons. They were playing at the Shepherd's Bush Empire theater in London, England. With the potential U.S. invasion of Iraq dominating the headlines, Maines offered a short monologue before introducing their song "Travelin' Soldier."

"Just so you know, we're on the good side with y'all. We do not want this war, this violence, and we're ashamed that the president of the United States is a Texan," she said.

Maines's remark sparked a great outcry across the United States. There were heated conversations on talk shows. There were endless newspaper columns arguing about what she had said. Many people wondered: Had the Dixie Chicks defamed America? Was this an act of treason?

The statement made in London sent shockwaves throughout the music industry as well. Some radio stations boycotted the Dixie Chicks' music. Their album sales dropped. And there was a provocative *Entertainment Weekly* cover on May 2, 2003, of the three bandmembers, naked except for inky black words painted on their skin: "traitors," "boycott," and "opinionated," among others. When the band sent in a donation to the American Red Cross for one million dollars, it was refused.

One month after the London show, journalist Diane Sawyer interviewed Maines on *Good Morning America*. She apologized for her words because they were disrespectful, but she didn't back away from the intent. As Maines had done all throughout her career, she didn't give in completely. "My apology was for the words that I used, but not for the motivation behind the words and for my beliefs," she said, as reported on CNN.

Sawyer grilled Maines further and turned on the other Dixie Chicks. When Maguire objected to Sawyer's query about what she would recommend be done about Iraq, Sawyer, according to *Salon* magazine, retorted, "If you're going to criticize the president for his own decision, you'd better have your own."

The backlash against the band continued. Two disc jockeys were suspended for playing the Dixie Chicks' music. There was booing at the Academy of Country Music Awards. When the Chicks went on the road, there were death threats against them, and, as a result, they hired around-the-clock security. Concertgoers had to walk through metal detectors. *Salon* reported that a DJ in San Antonio, Texas, suggested that a posse should "straighten Maines out," and an unidentified man in South Carolina said, "Anyone who thinks about going to that concert ought to be ready, ready, ready to run away from it."

Despite the ferocious outcry, the Chicks were able to laugh. At a VH1 awards ceremony in 2003, Maines joked (as quoted on CNN), "There's an old Texas expression that says if you don't have anything nice to say about someone, then go to London and say it in front of 2,000 people."

Chapter Four

Rebound

On March 16, 2006, the Dixie Chicks released the single "Not Ready to Make Nice" from their new album, *Taking the Long Way*. It addressed the political controversy that swirled around them after the statement made at their London concert. It also mentioned the death threats. "Not Ready to Make Nice" was their first single since the controversy. They wondered: Would it be well received? Would people take them seriously?

For the first time, they wrote or cowrote every song on the album. And to stack the deck in their favor, the Chicks hired producer Rick Rubin, who had revived the careers of music veterans Johnny Cash and Neil Diamond. Through his influence, *Taking the Long Way* was more rock-oriented. To the Chicks' surprise, the album sold 526,000 copies in its first week.

Producer Rick Rubin was a miracle man who helped the Dixie Chicks make a comeback.

There was also tenderness on the album that had nothing to do with politics. The song "Silent House" portrayed a woman with Alzheimer's disease. The straight-forward ballad "Easy Silence" featured a low-key rhythm guitar accentuated by Maguire's sharp fiddle. "Lullaby" created a dreamlike atmosphere with an eight-note melody repeated over nearly six minutes.

The Chicks were back in the game. They set forth on the Accidents & Accusations Tour. While ticket sales in Canada were strong, many American shows were canceled and relocated. But there were also innovations: The Chicks were the first band to have an embedded blogger on tour.

In 2006, the group released the documentary *Dixie Chicks: Shut Up or Sing*. The film followed the group from 2003 to 2006. It depicted stark moments on the Chicks' tour, including the death threats. In one moment, Maines examines a note that reads, "Natalie Maines will be shot dead Sunday, July 6, in Dallas, Texas." The police track down the subject and Maines replies, "He's kind of cute. He is. He's a good-looking guy."

But the Chicks still carried the burden of past mishaps. NBC refused to carry an ad for the film. Robison noted on *The Charlie Rose Show* that when the film was tested in Kansas City, "people were still calling us traitors and all the things they called us three years ago, and they had a hard time. They couldn't even get people to watch. So, it's still very divided."

Nevertheless, *Taking the Long Way* had earned the Dixie Chicks additional Grammy Award nominations. And much to everyone's surprise, they took home five Grammies. The Chicks swept up, winning awards for Album of the Year, Song of the Year, Record of the Year, Best Country Album, and Best Country Performance by a Duo or Group with Vocal. Rubin was recognized as Producer of the Year. These were more Grammies than the group had won for any album in their entire career.

The Decisions That Make a Career

The Dixie Chicks had walked down a long, hard road. They may no longer be the hottest act in country music, and they may not be

The Chicks regained their momentum, winning a Best Country Album Grammy for *Taking the Long Way.*

selling albums with the same blockbuster sales figures. But they have emerged from the 2003 incident with their integrity intact. *Taking the Long Way* only went double platinum, but it was a huge success in Canada. It also did very well in Australia, finishing at the 2006 End of the Year Country Charts in the number-one spot.

The Chicks had fought hard for their success, and they fought even harder to keep some scrap of it after the Bush controversy. Today, some country radio stations still refuse to put their music into heavy rotation. Yet, the band has never backed down. They've stayed true to their talent and to their collective voice. If fame and fortune had been the initial objectives, the Dixie Chicks have perhaps earned a more enduring and valuable achievement through their stubborn, spirited insistence on an honest and courageous integrity.

Timeline

1982–1988 Martie and Emily Erwin entertain audiences in the Blue Night Express.

1989 An early version of the Dixie Chicks forms, with the band playing on sidewalks in Dallas, Texas.

1995 Singer Laura Lynch is replaced by Natalie Maines.

1997 The Chicks begin recording *Wide Open Spaces*.

1998 *Wide Open Spaces* sells more than twelve million copies, becoming one of the fifty all-time best-selling albums in America.

2001 The Dixie Chicks sing "I Believe in Love" in a benefit concert shortly after the September 11, 2001, terrorist attacks.

2002 The band enters into a lawsuit with Sony. They release *Home*, an independently produced album.

2003 The Dixie Chicks perform "The Star-Spangled Banner" at Super Bowl XXXVII; Maines publicly criticizes U.S. president George W. Bush at a concert in London, England, starting a global controversy.

2006 The documentary *Dixie Chicks: Shut Up and Sing* is released.

2007 At the Grammy Awards, the Dixie Chicks win all five categories that for which they are nominated.

Discography

1990 *Thank Heavens for Dale Evans* (Little Red Hen)

1992 *Little Ol' Cowgirl* (Little Red Hen)

1993 *Shouldn'ta Told You That* (Little Red Hen)

1998 *Wide Open Spaces* (Sony)

1999 *Fly* (Sony)

2002 *Home* (Sony)

2003 *Top of the World Tour: Live* (Sony)

2006 *Taking the Long Way* (Sony)

Glossary

bluegrass A form of American roots music inspired by immigrants from the British Isles. In bluegrass, each of the instruments takes a turn at playing a melody and other instruments improvise around this main melody.

dobro A special lap steel guitar with a unique resonator invented in 1928 by the Dopyera brothers.

Grammy Awards Annual awards presented by the National Academy of Recording Arts and Sciences; considered to be the top music industry awards.

Lilith Fair A concert tour that ran between 1997 and 1999, designed to feature all-women bands; it was organized by Sarah MacLachlan.

mandolin A thin-necked instrument first introduced in Naples, Italy. It features a hollow wooden body and usually only four strings.

The Prairie Home Companion Live radio variety show hosted by Garrison Keillor; one of the first major venues for the Dixie Chicks.

rhinestone A colorless artificial gem made of paste or glass, often cut to sparkle like a diamond.

Shepherds Bush Empire Famed music venue in West London where Natalie Maines spoke out against U.S. president George W. Bush.

western swing A combination of country, jazz, and pop aimed at dancers and introduced in small town dance halls in the 1920s and 1930s.

For More Information

Billboard magazine
P.O. Box 15158
North Hollywood, CA 91615
Web site: http://www.
   billboard.com
Billboard magazine is the
   world's premier music
   publication.

Nielsen SoundScan Canada
111 Richmond Street West
Suite 1501
Toronto, ON M5H 2G4
Canada
Web site: http://www.
   soundscan.com
Nielsen SoundScan is a system
   that tracks music sales
   throughout the United
   States and Canada.

Sony BMG Music
   Entertainment, Inc.
555 Madison Avenue
New York, NY 10022-3211
Web site: http://www.
   sonybmg.com
Sony BMG Music Entertainment
   is a global record label.

Web Sites

Due to the changing nature of
Internet links, Rosen Publishing
has developed an online list of
Web sites related to the subject
of this book. This site is
updated regularly. Please use
this link to access the list:

http://www.rosenlinks.com/
   cmtm/dich

For Further Reading

Collins, Ace. *All About the Dixie Chicks*. New York, NY: St. Martin's Griffin, 1999.

Dickerson, James L. *Dixie Chicks: Down-Home and Backstage*. Dallas, TX: Taylor Trade Publishing, 2000.

Gerding Scholten, Kristi. *When Art and Celebrity Collide: Telling the Dixie Chicks to "Shut Up and Sing."* Saarbrucken, Germany: VDM Verlag, 2007.

Gray, Scott. *Chicks Rule: The Story of the Dixie Chicks*. New York, NY: Ballantine Books, 1999.

Seminara-Kennedy, Concetta. *The Dixie Chicks*. Philadelphia, PA: Chelsea House Publishers, 2002.

Smith Weber, Terri. *Dixie Chicks*. Dallas, TX: Panda Publishing, 2003.

Tracy, Kathleen. *The Dixie Chicks*. Toronto, Canada: ECW Press, 2000.

Bibliography

Bryant, Helen. "A Ground-Breaking Celebration." *Dallas Morning News*, November 16, 1995, p. 45A.

Bryant, Helen. "Guy Likes Three-Party System." *Dallas Morning News*, January 18, 1995, p. 25A.

The Charlie Rose Show. "Dixie Chicks." PBS, November 20, 2006.

Clark, Renee. "The Dixie Chicks: Blazing Happy Trails with a Unique Mix." *Dallas Morning News*, March 9, 1991, p. 5C.

Clark, Renee. "Local Heroes: Can the Dixie Chicks Make It in the Big Time?" *Dallas Morning News*, March 1, 1992, p. 16.

Corcoran, Michael. "Chicks Click—Sort Of." *Dallas Morning News*, March 30, 1992, Home, p. 21A.

Harris, Paul A. "A New Swing in Dixie Chicks Dallas Band Is Trading in Some of Its Bluegrass Licks for a Texas Sound." *St. Louis Post-Dispatch*, April 3, 1992, p. 4F.

Morgan, Kendall. "Vintage Western Wears Well on the Dixie Chicks." *Dallas Morning News*, October 14, 1992, p. 6E.

Wooley, John. "Dixie Chicks Hatch Back-to-Roots Country Style." *Tulsa World*, November 26, 1996, p. D2.

Index

About the Author

Brett Mitchells is an investigative journalist living in New York. He has covered local politics for many newspapers. His hobbies include fishing, trainspotting, and landscape painting.

Photo Credits

Cover, pp. 1, 8, 20, 34 © Getty Images; pp. 4–5, 9, 23, 38, 40 © WireImage/ Getty Images; pp. 13, 25, 31 © The Everett Collection; p. 29 © AFP/Getty Photos.

Designer: Gene Mollica; **Editor:** Peter Herman; **Photo Researcher:** Marty Levick